I AM A GUY FROM A PLACE, CHARM CITY BIPPER,
QUI$ THE VNDL, MARQUIS IS THE NAME MY MAMA GAVE ME.

ONE DAY MADE BETTER IS MANY DAYS MADE GREATER,
I'M UPLIFTING YOU TO BE IN A WORLD THAT CARES,
IF I KEEP IT TO MYSELF I THINK THAT THAT'S UNFAIR,
THE JOY I'VE BEEN GIVEN IS BEST WHEN SHARED.

VISIONARIE$ NEVER DIE LEGEND$ $URVIVE
THROUGH THE SEEDS WE SOW DAILY
WE GET BETTER WITH TIME.
WISHING YOU
PEACE, PROSPERITY, AND MANY BLESSINGS.

PLANT A SEED

ACTIONS SPEAK LOUDER THAN WORDS.
NO MATTER HOW PRETTY YOU SPEAK
YOUR NOUNS AND YOUR VERBS.
MAKE SURE THEY'RE TRUE
AND THE FRUITS OF YOUR WORKS,
ARE SHOWN THROUGH THE WORDS YOU
CHOOSE TO DISPERSE.

**ACTIONS SPEAK LOUDER
THAN WORDS**

YOU CANNOT DISCOVER
SOMETHING THAT HAS ALREADY EXISTED.
YOU FOUND GOD,
BUT YOU AREN'T
THE FIRST ONE WHO DID IT.
IT'S A FLAWED PREMISE.
HE WASN'T HIDING.
YOU WERE TOO DISTRACTED
BY THE FILTH THAT YOU LIE IN.

I FOUND GOD

I AM GRATEFUL
FOR BLESSINGS I HAVE NOT YET SEEN.
I KNOW THAT MY BLESSINGS ARE ALL WITHIN ME.
A SPIRIT OF GIVING
HAS ALWAYS BROUGHT MUCH MORE.
I CANNOT LOVE WHAT IS MINE
HAVING HATRED FOR YOURS.
I AM GRATEFUL FOR WAKING
AND GRATEFUL SOME MORE
THANKFUL I'M ABLE TO HONOR THE SOURCE
THANKFUL FOR PURPOSE, LOVE, WISDOM, AND PEACE
GRATEFUL FOR VISION AND TO LIVE OUT MY DREAMS

GRATEFUL

PEACE IS A CHOICE,
A WAY TO BE.
IF I TRY AND I SEEK
IT JUST KEEPS
ESCAPING ME.
IT'S NOT A PLACE
THOUGH IT IS A STATE TO ENTER.
BUT ONLY AFTER
WORRY, FEAR, AND DOUBT
ARE SURRENDERED.

EVERYDAY I'M POWERED BY FAITH.

I CHOOSE PEACE

YOU'VE JUDGED WITHOUT KNOWING.
YOU'VE JUDGED, BUT FEAR JUDGMENT.
YOU'VE JUDGED AND CRITIQUED THINGS YOUR HEART IS IN LOVE WITH.
WHAT HAS THAT BROUGHT YOU? WHAT HAS THAT LEFT YOU?
YOU WANT TO BE FAVORED, BUT YOU DON'T ACCEPT YOU.
YOU DON'T RESPECT YOU. GOING BACK ON YOUR WORD.
IF YOU'RE HONEST
YOU THINK STRESS IS WHAT YOU DESERVE.
YOU CAN DO SO MUCH. YOU CAN BE MUCH MORE.
CHECK THAT EGO.
IT WON'T SERVE YOU MOVING FORWARD.
CHECK THAT PRIDE. THAT'S FOR OTHERS TO HAVE FOR YOU.
IF YOU'RE REAL YOU'LL RISE
AND THERE'S NOTHING MAN CAN DO.
YOU'LL DO THE WORK.
YOU'LL PROVE YOUR WORTH.
YOU WILL FREE YOURSELF.
RELEASE JUDGMENT TO FREE OTHERS
IN NEED OF HELP.

YOU'VE JUDGED

MAY NOT CHANGE THE WORLD, BUT I'LL SURELY PLANT A SEED.
IT STARTED WITH A VISION IN A SPACE THAT CAN'T BE SEEN.
THE ARROGANCE OF MAN IS STOPPING MAN FROM BEING FREE.
BOUND AND CHAINED TO IDOLS AND FALSE SYSTEMS OF BELIEF.
CAN ONLY SPEAK FOR ME.
I AFFIRM THAT IT IS POSSIBLE.
WITH THE WAY MY MIND IS SET, MY MOVEMENT IS UNSTOPPABLE.
WON'T FOCUS ON LACK
OR THINGS I DO NOT HAVE,
THAT TREE BEARS ROTTEN FRUIT
FROM THAT THERE'S NOTHING TO BE HAD.

DONE WITH LOOKING BACK WITH RESENTMENT FOR MY PAST,
MOVING FORWARD WITH A STANCE THAT'S POSITIVE,
I COMMAND, MYSELF BEFORE OTHERS,
TO BE THE BEST THAT I CAN BE.
EVERYDAY I'M IN THIS WORLD BEING WHAT
EYE WANT TO SEE.

MAY NOT CHANGE THE WORLD

I WON'T COMPLAIN ABOUT PAINS I'VE KNOWN.
I LOVE THE PAINS THEY'VE MADE ME GROW.
I GET TO BE, GIVE AND RECEIVE,
WHAT'S MEANT FOR ME CONTINUALLY,
TO INFINITY.

SO I WON'T COMPLAIN
ABOUT WHAT IS SENT TO ME.
I WON'T COMPLAIN OR MAKE SPACE FOR MISERY.
EVERYDAY I GET IS A GIFT TUH ME.
CUZ I LOSS SOME FRIENDS, THAT
I WON'T GET TUH SEE UNTIL THE NEXT.
I DON'T HONOR FEAR.
I DON'T HONOR STRESS.
AND EVERY DAY I WAKE
I THANK THE ONE WHO LOVES ME BEST
I WON'T COMPLAIN.

THANK YOU GOD.

I WON'T COMPLAIN

I SEE WAY MORE IN DARKNESS,
STRUGGLES, PAINS, AND HARDSHIPS.
TO KNOW THE PEAKS AND VALLEYS
THE MAKINGS OF THIS ARTIST.
WITHOUT A PROOF OF CONCEPT
THEY JUST WON'T BELIEVE.
AND WHEN THE PROOF COMES OUT
THEY STILL WON'T BUY THE DREAM
UNTIL A BRIGHTER LIGHT SHINES.
BUT YOU KNEW THE TRUTH IN THE DARK.
THEY'RE USING THEIR MINDS.
THEY'RE NOT USING THEIR HEARTS.
NO MATTER WHO YOU ARE,
YOU MUST KNOW YOU MATTER,
IN BOTH THE PRAISE OF THEIR CHEERS,
AND THE REBUKE OF THEIR CHATTER.

I SEE WAY MORE IN DARKNESS

PRACTICE IS MY GIFT TO THE MAN I'LL BE TOMORROW.
WORKING THROUGH THE TRIALS DETACHING FROM THE SORROWS.
LET'S MAKE THE BEST OF ME BEFORE MY DAY OF RECKONING.
I APOLOGIZE FOR JUDGMENTS AND FOR NOT ACCEPTING THINGS
FOR WHAT THEY ARE.
A FOREIGN CAR WON'T SOLVE IT, BUT I WANT IT.
HAPPY AIN'T FROM WHERE I LIVE
OR WHAT'S PLACED IN MY STOMACH.
HAPPINESS HAD CAME FROM ALL MY GRATITUDE FOR NOTHING
I SMILE BIGGER AND LOVE HARDER
WHEN THERE'S LESS I'M WAKING UP WITH.
TRUST IT, TRUST IT, TRUST IT.
EVERY STEP OF THE PROCESS.
AND FOR EVERY BRIDGE THEY BURN
LET THEM THINK YOU'RE OBNOXIOUS.
THAT AIN'T YOUR PROBLEM.
LET THEM FEEL WHAT THEY MAY.
BECAUSE LIFE CHANGES DAILY
AND ALL THEM FEELINGS DECAY.

PRACTICE

I WISH A PEACEFUL REST TO THE BROTHERS WE HAVE LOST.
IT HURTS TO LOOK UP AND KNOW THAT THEY ARE GONE.
BROTHERS THAT DIDN'T SEE 30.
BROTHERS THE WORLD SAID WERE UNWORTHY.
NO MATTER WHAT HAT THEY WORE
THE NEWS ALWAYS HURTS ME.
MURDER IS A HEINOUS THEFT. ALWAYS HARD TO ACCEPT.
IT TAKES SO MUCH WITH ONE ACTION.
SO MUCH WE'RE NEVER GETTING BACK.
SO MUCH WE'LL NEVER GET TO HAVE.
SO MANY TEARS THAT GET SHED.
TO ALL THE ANGELS IN THE SKY
I WISH YOU A PEACEFUL REST.
FOR THE ONES YOU LEFT BEHIND
I PRAY TO GOD THAT THEY ARE BLESSED
WITH DRIER EYES AND SOBER MINDS
SO THEY CAN GO AND DO THEIR BEST.
THESE CYCLES MUST END. IT DOESN'T SIT RIGHT WITHIN
LOVE, LIGHT, AND PEACE
TO ALL OF MY FRIENDS.

PEACEFUL REST

THERE'S A WAR GOING ON OUTSIDE NO ONE IS SAFE FROM.
BLACK FOLKS DONE TOUCHED A BILL AND WE STILL AIN'T DONE
BLACK MAN LED CAPITOL HILL AND WE STILL AIN'T (WON) ONE
BLACKS WITH DEGREES AND SKILLS AND MAJOR INCOMES.

WAR GOING ON OUTSIDE OUR KIDS AIN'T READING.
KIDS TALKING SUICIDE WHAT'S THE REASON.
YOU FAKE IF CHOOSE TO HIDE THAT THERE IS TREASON.
BE THE CHANGE YOU SEEK TO FIND OR PLEASE STOP SPEAKING.

WAR GOING ON OUTSIDE NO ONE IS SAFE FROM.
FOOLS CAN FEEL THE TRUTH INSIDE, BUT THEY STILL MAKE FUN.
SEE IT WITH ALL OF THEIR EYES AND THEY STILL PLAY DUMB.
GOT EVERYTHING YOU DREAM TO BUY AND IT DON'T CHANGE MUCH.

STILL NIGGA. A PAIN I FEEL WITH CHA IF YEW FROM IT.
I KNOW WHO THEY EXCLUDE AND I KNOW THE ONES WHO DONE IT.
MAKING NO WAVES, WAITING FOR A CHANGE
MEANS IT AIN'T COMING.
YOU FALL FOR EVERYTHING
WHEN YOU STAND FOR NOTHING.

WAR

HAD TO DIE MANY TIMES TO LIVE THIS LIFE YOU SEE.
EGO HAD TO DIE TO LET MY SOUL BE FREE.
OPEN MIND, OPEN HEART
THAT MANY TIMES WAS TORN APART
I SAT WITH FEAR AND DEADLY THOUGHTS
ON MANY DAYS I PRAYED DISTRAUGHT.

WITH LITTLE FAITH STILL THINKING ME
WAS ALL THERE IS THAT WAS OF NEED
NO GRATITUDE JUST MAKE IT BE
A PLACE THAT'S FREE OF MISERY
AND FULL OF PLEASURE.

I COULDN'T SEE THE PART I PLAYED.
IF I WASN'T THE VICTIM
I WAS THE HERO FOR MY SAKE.
SELF RIGHTEOUSLY SPIRITUAL
THOUGHT I WAS BETTER THAN I WAS.
WISDOM WAS YELLING IN THE STREETS
AND I TURNED MY HEADPHONES UP.

EGO DEATH/ WISDOM IS YELLING

SOMETIMES ALL I NEED IS APPRECIATION.
ONE OF THOSE "I'M SO GLAD TO SEE YOU." "I'M HAPPY YOU MADE IT!"
FIRM DAPS, KIND HUGS, AND WARM SMILES.
TO FEEL LOVE AFTER GOING THOSE LONG MILES
OUT OF MY DARKNESS.
TO FEEL LIKE THEY KNOW WHERE MY HEART IS.
IT HASN'T BEEN EASY AND LORD KNOW THAT MY HEARTS BEEN
IN SO MANY WRONG PLACES
BUT PLEASE SAVE THE LONG FACES.
I'VE HAPPILY AWAKENED TO SEE THIS THING WE PARTAKE IN
STARTS IN THE MIND AND THE ACTIONS WE'RE MAKING
GOOD, BAD, OR INDIFFERENT
CREATE IT AND SHAPE IT.
SO... CHOOSE WISELY
AND PLEASE CHOOSE SLOWLY.
AND GIVE ME TRUE KINDNESS IF YOU FEEL LIKE YOU OWE ME.
CAUSE SOMETIMES ALL I NEED IS APPRECIATION
ONE OF THOSE "I SEE WHAT YOU DO
AND I GLADLY EMBRACE IT."
LOVE.

APPRECIATION

WHAT IS THE PURPOSE?
WHO DOES IT SERVE?
WHAT IS YOUR PURPOSE?
WHAT IS YOUR WORTH?
WHO DO YOU SERVE?
TEW WHOM, DO YEW BELONG?
IS THE PURPOSE TO SERVE SELF? IS SELF SERVICE WRONG?
WHAT'S A LIFE WITH NO PURPOSE? IS IT A LIFE?
IF YOU'VE GOT NO PURPOSE CAN YOU GIVE ADVICE?
WHEN YOU LIVE A WORTHY PURPOSE THERE IS NO DYING.
YOU LIVE ON FOREVER
THROUGH THE WORKS
YOU'VE SUPPLIED.
I WONDER SO OFTEN ABOUT THIS PURPOSE OF MINE.
THE FAITH I'VE COMPRISED
IN THE LIFE THAT I FIND.
REMAINING STEADFAST AND REMAINING ALIGNED
WITH THE ALMIGHTY POWER
OF THE MOST HIGH.

PURPOSE

I'VE CHANGED SO MUCH AND I CHANGED SO QUICK
THAT THERE ARE THINGS THAT HAPPEN
THAT I DON'T EVEN GET
I LET THINGS ROLL OFF AND TIME I ONCE SPENT
THINKING ABOUT WHAT COULD AND SHOULD BE
NO LONGER PAYS RENT,
IN MY MIND. I AM HAPPY.
IN WAYS THAT ARE HARD TO EXPLAIN.
ESPECIALLY TO PEOPLE WHO ALWAYS COMPLAIN.
I AM DROPPING THE BAGS.
I AM RELEASING THE PAST.
I HAVE FORGIVEN MYSELF.
I AM NOT LOOKING BACK
WITH RESENTMENT.
I LOOK BACK NOW UNDERSTANDING
THAT THEY ALL DID THEIR BEST
AND NO MATTER WHAT HAPPENED
I AM STILL HERE.
I MADE IT. I SURVIVED.
AND I WILL KEEP ON KEEPING ON
TIL I'M CALLED BY THE MOST HIGH

NEW ME

WE WANT TO KNOW WHY?

WHY DO WE GO THROUGH PAIN?

WHY DO WE HURT AND COMPLICATE SIMPLE THINGS?

LIFE COULD BE SIMPLE AND

LIFE COULD BE PLAIN.

WHY DO WE CARE ABOUT WHAT THEY WILL THINK?

WHEN IT'S NEGATIVE?

WHY DO WE FEEL LESSER THAN?

WHY DON'T YOU GIVE LOVE?

WHY IS THE SECONDHAND

TRAUMA

JUST AS BAD AND SOMETIMES WORSE?

WHY DO WE WANT TO KNOW?

WHAT DOES IT SERVE?

IT HASN'T SERVED ME

SOMETIMES KNOWING HURTS.

I DESPISE KNOWING TRIVIAL THINGS,

BUT NOT KNOWING MY WORTH.

WHY?

WHY?

SO SMART YOU'RE STUPID.
YOU CAN'T SEE THAT YOU'VE BECOME
ALL THE FOLKS YOU SAID YOU'D NEVER BE.
IT DIDN'T TAKE TOO MUCH,
EFFORT ON YOUR PART.
IT CAME SO NATURAL.
YOU HAD YOUR FOCUS ON WHAT WAS WRONG.
TELL ME WHO'S LAUGHING NOW?
CHANGE YOUR GAZE
TO CHANGE YOUR DAYS
FROM DAYS OF BITTERNESS AND FROWNS.
YOU'VE CRITICIZED.
YOU'VE LIVED A LIE.
I HOPE YOU GET IT NOW.
YOU ARE WHAT YOU SAY YOU AREN'T
CAUSE THAT IS ALL YOU KNOW.
JUDGING ALL THEIR WRONGS
IS NO RECIPE FOR GROWTH.

SO SMART

GIVE THEM THEIR FLOWERS WHEN THEY CAN SMELL THEM.
IF YOU LIKE WHAT YOU SEE YOU SHOULD TELL THEM.
IF YOU GOT TIME TO GIVE
GO AND HELP THEM.

GIVE THEM THEIR FLOWERS.
LET THEM KNOW THAT YOU FELT THEM.
LET THEM KNOW THAT YOU SEE THEM.
LET THEM KNOW THAT THEY'RE HEARD.
LET THEM KNOW THAT THEY MATTER
BEFORE THEY LEAVE FROM THIS EARTH.
DON'T WAIT TIL THERE'S
NO WAY LEFT TO GIVE THEM.

GIVE THEM THEIR FLOWERS
WHEN THEY CAN SMELL THEM AND FEEL THEM.

MAY THE FRUITS OF YOUR WORKS
NEVER GO ROTTEN.
AND WE HONOR THE ONES
THE WORLD HAS FORGOTTEN.

GIVE THEM THEIR FLOWERS

THIS LIFE IS EASY. WE MAKE IT HARD.
WE CHOOSE THINGS WE HATE
AND WE THINK WE'RE SO SMART.
SO SMART AND SO WISE LIVING MISERABLE LIVES.
DECEIVING OURSELVES CONTINUALLY DYING.
IN FEAR,
IN WORRY,
IN LUST,
IN PAIN.
JUDGING OURSELVES HOLDING FEELINGS OF SHAME.
DEALING WITH TRAUMAS.
COPING WITH HORRIBLE HABITS.
IGNORANT ABOUT WHO WE ARE.
TRYING TO SOLVE IT WITH MAGIC.
WISHING ON STARS.
READING THE CARDS.
HAVING FAITH WITH NO WORKS.
PART TIME BELIEVING IN GOD.
LIFE IS SO EASY, BUT WE MAKE IT HARD.
LIFE IS SO EASY, BUT WE MAKE IT HARD.

LIFE IS SO EASY

HOW ARE YOU?

I'M HERE.
I'M HERE AND GRATEFUL TO BE ABLE TO BE.
I'M HERE.
THERE'S FOLKS THAT DIDN'T WAKE FROM THEIR SLEEP.
I'M HERE.
IN A DAY FOLKS AIN'T MAKE IT TO SEE.
I'M HERE.
AND I'M GRATEFUL AND I'M THANKFUL FOR PEACE.
I'M HERE.
LORD KNOWS WHERE I COULD'VE BEEN.
I USED TO LOOK DOWN THEN WAS TOLD TO LOOK AGAIN.
I'M HERE.
AND IT'S A BLESSING TO BE.

LOVE TO ALL THE ONES
THAT SHARE THIS
BLESSING WITH ME.

I AM HERE

I AM NOT MY PAST
AND I TRULY MEAN IT.
I KNOW WHERE I WAS,
BUT TO MOVE FORWARD
I DON'T NEED IT.
I DON'T NEED THE LIMITS.
I DON'T NEED THE DOUBT.
I DON'T NEED THE SHAME.
I CAN LIVE WITHOUT
THE GUILT
AND THE PAIN OF MY STORY
AND STILL GIVE IT HONOR
AND STILL GIVE HIM GLORY.
GRATEFUL TO THE HIGHEST
I LET FAITH BE MY ARMOR.
NO WEAPON FORMED
AGAINST ME
SHALL
PROSPER TO HARM US.

I AM NOT MY PAST

I WAS MADE TO PRACTICE YOGA
IT'S ALWAYS BEEN IN ME.
I ENJOY THE ASANAS
AND ALL THAT THEY GIVE ME.
I ENJOY THE BREATH WORK AND I LOVE TO SIT.
I GIVE SO MUCH TO MYSELF
IT'S A BEAUTIFUL GIFT.

I FEEL JOY, I FEEL FREE, A DEEP BEAUTIFUL BLISS.
I CAN SEE MUCH FURTHER
THAN THE PLACE I'VE LIVED.
I CAN SEE MUCH FURTHER
THAN WHAT THEY SAY ABOUT IT.
I UNDERSTAND THINGS
THEY SAY ARE PROBLEMS.

I PUT THE SKILL INTO ACTION
I AM IN LOVE WITH THE PRACTICE.
I DEDICATE IT TO THE HIGHEST
MY FORTRESS, MY CAPTAIN.

YOGI

UPWARD AND ONWARD
TIME TO MOVE FORWARD.
WAITING FOR NO MAN
I AM THE SOURCE OF
THE LIFE
THAT I LIVE IN THIS WORLD.
POWERED BY GOD.
BLESSED WITH HIS WORKS.

UPWARD

GOD CAN HEAR YOU. HE IS ALWAYS NEAR YOU.
DOUBT WON'T SERVE YOU.
WHY ARE YOU FEARFUL?
DO NOT FRET.
THE LORD PROTECTS
ALL HIS CHILDREN.
EVERY BREATH IS BLESSED.
EVERY STEP IS BLESSED.
ALLOW HIM TO BE YOUR SOURCE.
BE ABOUT HIM IN THE WORLD AND IN YOUR DEEPEST CORE.
KEEP HIM FIRST
WITHIN THIS HOLY TEMPLE.
THAT HOLDS THE SPIRIT
THAT HE ASSEMBLED.

GOD CAN HEAR YOU

SAY IT LOUD AND KNOW WHY YOU SAY IT.
HE HAD A DREAM THAT'S NOT TO BE PLAYED WITH.
ALL THE BRICKS OUR ANCESTORS LAID
ON WHICH WE STAND.
BRING US POWER IN OUR PRESENT DAY
FEW THOUGHT WE WOULD HAVE.
THEY FOUGHT FOR US TO VOTE. THEY FOUGHT FOR US TO BE.
ALL THAT WE ARE AND ALL THAT YOU SEE.
THEY FOUGHT FOR YEARS. FOUGHT CONSISTENTLY.
SO DON'T YOU EVER DISRESPECT OUR HISTORY.
DO NOT WAIT FOR IT TO COME TO YOU.
DO NOT WAIT UNTIL YOU ARE COMFORTABLE.
GO NOW BECAUSE IF THEY WAITED
AND DID ONLY WHAT THEY WANTED TO.
THE DOORS WOULD STILL BE CLOSED ON MANY
THINGS WE LOVE TO DO.
RESPECT WHAT WE HAVE AND ALL THEY CHOSE TO STRUGGLE THROUGH.
DO NOT TAKE YOUR FREEDOMS FOR GRANTED.
MANY BLACK FOLKS DIED SO YOU COULD HAVE IT.

SAY IT LOUD

THANK YOU FOR THE WORDS YOU DIDN'T KNOW I NEEDED.
FOR LISTENING INTENTLY TO EVERY WORD I WAS SPEAKING.
FOR HAVING A MIND THAT'S OPEN AND FREE OF JUDGMENT.
AND KNOWING MY FLAWS, BUT NOT BASHING ME IN PUBLIC.
THANK YOU FOR SHOWING UP FOR ME AND MANY OTHERS.
THANK YOU TO MY FATHERS,
THANK YOU TO MY MOTHERS,
THANK YOU TO MY SISTERS,
THANK YOU TO MY BROTHERS,
THANK YOU TO THE HIGHEST
WHO'S ALWAYS KEEPING ME COVERED.

THANK YOU, I LOVE YOU.
BLESS YOUR HEART AND ALL YOUR WORKS.
YOU ARE NOT YOUR PAST.
LOVE DOES NOT HAVE TO BE EARNED.
PEACE CAN NOT BE SOUGHT.
LOVE AND PEACE ARE STATES OF BEING.
WE ARE EVERYTHING
WAY MORE THAN WHAT WE'RE SEEING.

THANK YOU

THANK YOU FOR THE WORDS YOU DIDN'T KNOW I NEEDED.
FOR SPEAKING ON WHAT EVERYONE WAS SEEING.
FOR SAYING I LOVE YOU, BUT ONLY WHEN YOU MEAN IT.
AND KEEPING MY SECRETS BETWEEN YOU AND JESUS.

FOR WHEN I THOUGHT I NEEDED MORE
AND YOU SAW WHAT I HAD.
AND I THOUGHT I COULD NOT GO ON
BUT YOU TOLD ME I CAN.

FOR GIVING ME CORRECTION
THAT HAS MADE ME BE A MAN
THAT KNOWS WISDOM FROM THE SOURCE
WILL BRING THE LIFE HE WANTS TO HAVE.

THANK YOU FOR THE LOVE
THANK YOU FOR BELIEVING.
THANK YOU FOR THE WORDS
YOU DIDN'T KNOW
I NEEDED.

THANK YOU PT.2

I AM NOT THAT DIAGNOSIS
I AM NOT THAT DAY. I AM NOT THAT MOMENT.
IT'S BEEN SEVEN YEARS OF HEALING
AND THE PRAYERS AND THE FOCUS
HAS BEEN ON DOING WHAT I'M TOLD BY GOD.
I KNOW Y'ALL GET SCARED, BUT PLEASE REMAIN CALM.
I AM A SPIRIT THAT CAN NOT BE BROKEN
I HAVE MADE IT THROUGH FIRE,
THROUGH FEAR, AND TROUBLING EMOTIONS
I'VE MADE IT OUT TO THE OTHER SIDE OF A STORM THAT WAS HEAVY
THERE WERE PEOPLE THERE WITH ME, BUT MOST OF THEM LEFT ME
I ASKED GOD TO REMOVE FOLKS THAT ARE NOT FOR ME
MOMENTS CAME AND THEY WENT RIGHT WITH THE PROPHECY
PEOPLE BLAME ME FOR THE WAYS THEY SHOW UP.
IT'S NO HARM. IT'S NO FOUL. I WILL ALWAYS SHOW LOVE.
IT'S JUST SO WILD HOW IT ALL PLAYS OUT.
IF YOU'RE WONDERING I'M GOOD AND KEEP MY NAME OUT YOUR MOUTH
IF YOU AIN'T SPEAKING ON IT
WITH LOVE OR SPEAKING IT TUH ME.
RESPECTFULLY

LETTER TO THE DOUBTER

❤ I SINCERELY THANK YOU FOR PURCHASING THIS BOOK. ❤

DM ME YOUR FAVORITE POEM
AND SAY "LOVE TO BIP".
MUCH MORE TO COME.
WE GON SHINE FOREVER.

BIP BIP

INSTAGRAM & TIK TOK: CHARMCITYBIPPER
YOUTUBE: A GUY FROM A PLACE

VISIONARIES NEVER DIE LEGENDS SURVIVE

Made in the USA
Middletown, DE
14 August 2023